BEI GRIN MACHT SICH IHR WISSEN BEZAHLT

- Wir veröffentlichen Ihre Hausarbeit,
  Bachelor- und Masterarbeit

- Ihr eigenes eBook und Buch -
  weltweit in allen wichtigen Shops

- Verdienen Sie an jedem Verkauf

Jetzt bei www.GRIN.com hochladen
und kostenlos publizieren

Florian Rübener

Violence on TV

How the American society deals with violence on TV

GRIN Verlag

Bibliografische Information der Deutschen Nationalbibliothek:

Die Deutsche Bibliothek verzeichnet diese Publikation in der Deutschen National-
bibliografie; detaillierte bibliografische Daten sind im Internet über http://dnb.d-
nb.de/ abrufbar.

Impressum:

Copyright © 2003 GRIN Verlag, Open Publishing GmbH
Druck und Bindung: Books on Demand GmbH, Norderstedt Germany
ISBN: 978-3-640-85388-5

Dieses Buch bei GRIN:

http://www.grin.com/de/e-book/163936/violence-on-tv

Montag, 10. Februar 2003   Englisch (LK)

Verfasst von:

Florian Rübener

<u>Facharbeit</u>

<u>Violence on TV – How the American society</u>

<u>deals with violence on TV</u>

Table of contents

Preface

A short look at television's history

It was 1926 when the Scotsman John Baird (1888-1946) presented the first television broadcast and when the American W.K. Zworykin[1] (1889-1982) invented the first electronically working television set nearly at the same time, nobody could ever imagine the future dimensions of that big, black and unwieldy box. But since the regularly broadcasting of TV-shows in 1935, the television became a steady rising supplementation of people's life all over the world. Although television sets got smaller and smaller, the meaning of that medium was never bigger as today.

(source: Das große Ravensburger Lexikon-Band 2, © 1992 by Ravensburger Buchverlag Otto Maier GmbH)

---

[1] Zworykin came originally from Russia.

3

While in 1950 only 10% of American families had a television, today 99% do. In fact more families own a television than a phone[1]! Whether sport-events, rock-concerts or dramas, for people in our time the television is an irreplaceable and untiring source of entertainment. Supplying people with news from every place on earth, the television became also one of the most important deliverer of information and knowledge.

The part television takes up in our society is much bigger than we expect it to be. The times when television just entertained us are already over; today we are also informed, inspired and influenced by that medium. Television became an important addition to our everyday life; it keeps us informed about events that happen all over the world and helps us to shape an opinion by supplying us with information.

The things we see on TV often inspire us and sometimes we might be able to transfer specific occurrences on our own life.

1.Introduction

1.1 Explaining the topic

The topic I chose for my term paper is "Violence on TV-How the American society deals with violence on TV". So what does that mean exactly? Violence on TV is (too often because of current events) an often-discussed topic. Scientists, media experts, politicians and TV-station bosses are quarrelling for years now about the responsibility of television and its influence on the watcher.

---

[1] See Mediascope: American Public Opinion on Media Violence, 1993

Acts of violence or criminal actions are often blamed on TV, parents are afraid of the bad influence that medium might have and violent behaviour caused by television-violence.

1.2 Why this topic?

I think the question about the responsibility of the media, in this case of television, in our modern society is very interesting and of course important. With this term paper I want to explain the situation in America; what the dimensions of violence on TV are, how the society deals with that topic, what scientists say about it, if there is a connection between real-life violence and televised aggression and why there are so many violent programs on TV. The key-question I want to answer is: "Is it justified to blame the television for violent behaviour?"

1.2.1 What material will be used?

The difficulty about this topic is that it deals with the American society. At first it was not easy to find some useful material, because all books to get deal with the situation in Germany.

I decided to search for material on the Internet and the mass of information about violence on TV in America was overwhelming. The material I chose comes from two objective, non-partisan and non-profit research and educational organizations, "The Centre for Media and Public Affairs[1]" and "Mediascope"[2].

---

[1] CMPA was founded in 1985.
[2] Mediascope was founded in 1992.

Those so-called "watchdog-organizations" promote issues of social relevance within the entertainment industry. They publish studies and reports on a steady basis to inform (or sometimes warn) the American public about television and other media. Topics those organizations deal with are for example media ratings, children's television and media violence. The material I took from them contains most studies and reports about the dimensions of TV-violence and the context in which violence is presented.

Further material was taken from the "American Psychological Association"-website, a scientific organization that represents psychology in America and the books "Sündenbock Frensehen?" by Georg Kofler[1] and "Kinder und neue Medien" by Patricia M. Greenfield[2], an American psychology-professor from the university of California in Los Angeles.

Some material is from an article published in the "Los Angeles Times" on March 21st, 2002[3].

2. Violence on TV and its effect on the watcher

2.1 How is violence presented on TV and in what dimensions?

Violence on TV is an often-discussed topic. If we take a look at the extent of violence, we see on TV, this fact is not very surprising.

In 1992 the "Centre for Media and Public Affairs"[4] published a study, which based on the results of analysing 10 channels[5] for 24 hours on a

---

[1] The book was not written by Georg Kofler himself, it contains different texts from different authors, which were collected by Kofler in this book.
[2] The book used is the German translated version.
[3] Los Angeles Times: Sex and Violence on TV: It's on the Decline Study Finds, by Megan Garvey, March 21, 2002.
[4] Compare 1.2.1: What material was used?
[5] The ten channels chosen included three major networks, public television and some popular cable channels.

typical American day[1]. The results of that study are really appalling; in the 24 hours analysed there were 1846 scenes showing individual acts of violence, 175 scenes of violence resulting in the death of people, 389 scenes of serious assault[2], 673 scenes of punching, slapping or pushing and another 588 scenes of gunplay or threats including a weapon.

More than half of all dramas, comedies, movies and music videos contained violent scenes, the study concluded. The really alarming result is that forty-six percent of all television violence took place in children's cartoons! That means that the average American child will witness over 200.000 acts of violence until he/she reached age 18.

The extent of violence on TV is huge, but what about the context in which violence is presented? In 1996 the "National Television Violence Study", issued by Mediascope[3], was published. Mediascope analysed 2,500 hours of cable and broadcast program and specialized on the way of violence presentation. Although Mediascope did not single out a particular show, it warns that the context in which violence was portrayed can be dangerously misleading to viewers.

Violence was too often glorified and the real consequences were hardly shown. Violence was presented as a justified way of solving problems and three-quarters of the shows with violent content demonstrated unpunished violence. Children's programs were least likely to show the long-term consequences of violence and portrayed violent actions in a humorous fashion sixty-seven percent of the time. When persons were attacked or hurt, they were not shown experiencing pain.

So violence is not only shown in huge amount, it is also demonstrated in an unrealistic and harmless way.

---

[1] Typical means there was no unusual event of civil disorder on the news and no atypical movies were broadcasted.
[2] For example war scenes or scenes with masses of people fighting each other.
[3] The Mediascope study was sponsored by the cable industry and conducted across four universities.

2.2 The influence of TV-violence on the watcher

Because of that increased violence demonstration on TV, the apprehension of the watchers increases too.

"All that violence on TV is bad for you!" or "It's all the televisions fault!" are often heard statements, mostly expressed by concerned parents who are worried about the bad influence television might have on their children. But is this anxiety justified or completely unnecessary? How dangerous is TV-violence?

Many scientists, for example psychiatrists and media experts, handled with that question and published studies and reports. Although some of them are over ten years old, the results don't vary much from current studies. Because all experts agree that TV-violence can be a serious threat for the watcher! Psychological research has shown three major effects on seeing violence on television.

Because of the steady repetition of specific violent actions watchers, especially children, may become less sensitive to it.[1] That means they are getting numb to violence and violent behaviour, they show less compassion for people suffering or feeling pain and they lose the ability to realize the consequences of violence against persons. The second effect concerns especially younger watchers. If children see much aggression, anger and assault on TV they may become more fearful of the world around them and show timid and shy behaviours towards other individuals[2]. They get afraid that the scenes they saw on different shows might happen to them and their view on the world is shaped badly. But this effect vanishes mostly when the children get older because the experiences they make by growing up change their attitude again.

---

[1] See American Psychological Association: Big World Small Screen: The Role of Television in American Society, 1985
[2] See American Psychological Association: Big World Small Screen: The Role of Television in American Society, 1985

8

The third effect the research has shown seems to justify the blaming of television. "Children may be more likely to behave in aggressive or even harmful ways towards others!"[1]

Studies have shown that children, who watch a lot violent shows, even just funny cartoons, were more likely to hit their playmates, argue and quarrel, disobey rules and leave tasks unfinished. That's because they "learn" that violence is normal[2].

Although these are scientific proved facts, psychiatrists warn to judge television to soon. Because it is also proven that that the influence family, friends and the whole social environment have on some person is much bigger than the TV ones[3]. These three effects concern not every child in the same way; children growing up in an intact family are less threatened than children experiencing aggression in reality too.

3. How the society deals with televised violence

3.1 Where the violence comes from

Why is there so much violence on TV? The answer on this question is quiet simple, violence means profit!

Profit is the engine driving the entertainment industry. Broadcasters have to catch the audiences' attention to reach them with their programs, and programs have to stimulate them to keep them tuned in. But because of the lots of stimulation on TV it is increasingly difficult to capture and hold the attention of the public. So the task for the broadcasters is to find something that stands out from the crowd.

---

[1] American Psychological Association: Big World Small Screen: The Role of Television in American Society, 1985
[2] Compare 1.1: How is violence presented on TV and in what dimensions?
[3] See Michael Kunczik:Sündenbock Fernsehen?,Berlin 1995, p.47.

Violence definitely can do that! Violence gets our attention. Because of that, violence has become a favourite content of TV-shows and an often-used gimmick by those who want the public's attention.

Because of that increased violence presentation, the audience becomes desensitised to the level of violence over time and so the violence must reach a higher level to capture the watcher again. And as the public gets tired of that level too, the shows will become more violent again. The consequence of that is an audience, which gets increasingly resistant by increased violent demonstration[1].

3.2 What are the public's reactions?

So the broadcasters give the audience just what it wants right[2]? False! In fact the public seems to get tired of violent programs and shows with aggressive content.

A study, published by Mediascope in 1993, shows that about 72% of the American public finds that television entertainment has too much violence[3]. This result can have different reasons, maybe TV-violence got to its limit and there is nothing stimulating left so the audience starts to get bored.

A quiet more sensible reason would be that the public realized the menace of TV-violence and got afraid of increased real-life violence caused by aggression shown on television. This seems to be the reason indeed!

Because the Mediascope study shows also that 80% of Americans think television is harmful. The number of those who believe it is very harmful increased from 26% in 1983 to 47% in 1993. Of those surveyed, 53 % are sure that viewing portrayals of violence in television make people more likely to behave in a violent way.

---

[1] See Michael Kunczik: Sündenbock Fernsehen?, Berlin 1995, p.31.
Compare 1.2: The influence of TV-violence on the watcher
[2] Compare 3.1: Where the violence comes from
[3] See Mediascope: American Public Opinion on Media Violence, 1993

Violent programs are getting more and more unpopular and half of all parents polled who had children aged eight to thirteen said that they turn of the TV or switch the channel to prevent a child from seeing something aggressive. Of course we don't have to wait long for a reaction from those who are living from TV viewing figures, the broadcasters.

The Centre for Media and Public Affairs found that serious violent material fell by 17% from the 1998-99 TV season to the 200-01 seasons[1]. The centre's president S. Robert Lichter said: "You can't know the future, but this is the first bit of good news in a while […] whether it is invisible ink that will disappear, we'll wait to see."[2]

4. Solutions

4.1 Is it justified blaming the television?

If we look at the scientific facts[3] the answer on this question is: "Partly!" Because it is proven that there is some kind of influence on the watcher, that children may become aggressive because of the things they see on TV, but television is not the only factor shaping some persons attitude[4].

Further social experiences and the family situation are responsible for the development of some person, rather than the media[5].

The execution of violence is normally suppressed by hindrances for example the fear of punishment and revenge, guilty consciences and fear[6].

---

[1] See Los Angeles Times: Sex and Violence on TV: It's on the Decline Study Finds, by Megan Garvey, March 21, 2002.
[2] Los Angeles Times: Sex and Violence on TV: It's on the Decline Study Finds, by Megan Garvey, March 21, 2002.
[3] Compare 2.2: The influence of TV-violence on the watcher
[4] Compare 2.2: The influence of TV-violence on the watcher
[5] See Michael Kunczik:Sündenbock Fernsehen?,Berlin 1995, p.47.
[6] See Michael Kunczik:Sündenbock Fernsehen?,Berlin 1995, p.45

The harmless and unrealistic image of violence on TV[1] can make children forget these hindrances and assure them that violence is normal. But that doesn't count for every child! Not every child kills somebody after he/she watched a violent movie, the environment in which the child grows up influences and shapes his/her character much more than the television does.

4.2 What parents can do to protect their children

When worried parents blame the television for influencing their children in a bad way, they forget mostly that they have the possibility to weak that influence a lot.

Actually parents can influence what their children learn from TV by supplying their child with information while watching television[2]. Parents have to explain different coherences and that the actors don't really get hurt or killed and that such violence causes pain or death in real life[3]. Television influences children only in a bad way, if the child has no experiences with the specific topic yet[4]. So parents have to talk about with their children what they just saw and to tell them that such behaviour is not the best way of solving a problem.

4.2.1 My personal view

School shootings have been a major negative factor in our society lately, and since that one in Erfurth we know that its not one of those typical American-high school problems.

---

[1] Compare 2.1: How is violence presented on TV and in what dimensions?
[2] See Patricia M. Greenfield: Kinder und neue Medien, München 1987, p.53
[3] Compare 2.1: How is violence presented on TV and in what dimensions?
[4] See Patricia M. Greenfield: Kinder und neue Medien, München 1987, p.54

Every time one[1] happens it sparks a debate. Teachers, scientists, politicians and parents all discuss what causes violence and (extreme) aggressive behaviour and who's to blame.

Blame the TV. Why not? Television is well known for demonstrating violence in huge dimensions, there could possibly be a link between that and real-life violence. However the television is inspired by reality and shows only a reflection of society, showcasing violence that happens in real life. How can politicians say television teaches violence while they are preparing for a war against Iraq? Who is the one demonstrating violence[2] as a way of solving problems?

Television is not supposed to educate children and to tell them what's wrong or right, it is supposed to entertain people! If parents suspect the television to influence their children in a negative way and they don't want them watching violent shows, fine, have parental controls or whatever.

However, I think if children are never exposed to violence and what goes on outside of their houses, they might grow up very sheltered and naive, and may not be able to handle with violence they see.

Blame the parents. This is the most widely used argument, and probably the most important one. Parents should know what's going on with their children, they should notice if their child is about to kill his/her classmates, right? No! Of course parents can't be everywhere and they are not supposed to know and see everything their child does.

So who is to blame then? Teachers? Music? Marilyn Manson[3]? It may be all or none of the arguments presented. Every person driven to think that violence is a solution, obviously has some big emotional problems, caused by many sorts of things.

It could be violence on TV, it could be the parents, and it could be bad experiences made in life. However, one thing isn't to be blamed, its more or less society as whole. We should focus on solving the problem, rather than

---

[1] Or a comparable tragedy.
[2] In this case war.
[3] Famous shock-rock star that is notorious for his aggressive lyrics and performances. Manson's music was blamed for the school shooting in Littleton. His name contains Marilyn Monroe and Charles Manson, a notorious serial killer.

blaming a single group. Parents, teachers and politicians should teach children that violence is never the answer.

If you want something caused by society to stop, the society must change.

5. List of sources

The following sources were used for the material from which this term paper was created.

American Psychological Association: Big World Small Screen: The Role of Television in American Society, ©Washington D.C. 1985, www.apa.org

Centre for Media and Public Affairs: Study about the dimensions of TV-violence, ©1992, www.cmpa.com

Das große Ravensburger Lexikon-Band 2, ©by Ravensburger Buchverlag Otto Maier GmbH,1992

Garvey, Megan: Sex and Violence on TV: It's on the Decline Study Finds, ©Los Angeles Times, Los Angeles, March 21, 2002, www.losangelestimes.com

Greenfield, Patricia M: Kinder und neue Medien, ©München 1987

Kofler, Georg: Sündenbock Fernsehen?,©Berlin 1995

Mediascope: American Public Opinion on Media Violence, © Washington D.C. 1993, www.mediascope.org

Mediascope: National Television Violence Study, © Washington D.C. 1996, www.mediascope.org

Written by Florian Rübener, © Dinslaken Sunday, 09 February 2003